STEP UP

MOLLY ANN LUNA

Copyright © 2020 Team Luna Productions

All rights reserved.

ISBN: 9798656215183

Book design by Team Luna Productions

www.TeamLunaProductions.com

DEDICATION

To the Legacy Leaders who are building True Wealth for their future generations to come

ACKNOWLEDGMENTS

Team Luna, thank you for your endless encouragement & support.

CONTENTS

INTRODUCTION 1

1 : MONETIZE YOUR EXPERTISE 5

2 : ONLINE INCOME STREAMS 17

3 : BRANDING YOU 25

4 : BUSINESS MODELS THAT WORK 35

5 : WEBINARS 43

6 : LIVE TRAINING 49

7 : GETTING PAID TO COACH 55

ABOUT THE AUTHOR 63

INTRODUCTION

Here's the deal, whether you realize it or not, you are an expert in at least one area of knowledge. It doesn't matter what it is. Maybe you know how to organize a messy house a little better than everybody else, perhaps you know how to cook, maybe you've discovered a way to burn fat more efficiently or how to trade the market. Regardless of who you are, your background, education, or experiences you have at least one thing that you can get paid for to teach others.

Your unique interests and experiences are what makes hanging out with new people so rewarding. Getting the opportunity to share ideas and 'see' the world from another perspective through the power of storytelling is what connects us. It's in our nature to share and grow, so there lie the makings of the multi-million-dollar industry, coaching.

Here's the thing, I bet that you're good at many things. When you can drill down on a few key areas, where you're still curious to discover more, you've found your coaching 'lane.' Once you've identified that you can start your business, yes, it is possible to earn a living by learning new things and teaching them.

You can think of online coaching as an extension of continued learning. It's a way to help educate people on things that they didn't already know. With online education in the form of coaching, typically, one does not receive some sort of certification or diploma, but the essence is the same.

At this very moment, people are typing into their search bar questions to help provide answers to their problems. And the cool thing is that they're willing to pay you for those answers. The world we live in is extensively expert-based, and there is a tremendous need for coaches like you to step up and teach.

Why? Well, the internet has an alluring, but a strange effect on people. As more and more information is uploaded online, more than ever, people feel isolated and alienated. People seek leaders, like you who are willing to step up, and experts they can trust.

Now, if you're feeling a little resistance around becoming a leader or that the word expert feels too strong, please don't let these titles overwhelm you. Leadership is a learnable skill, something that we cover the in-depth inside of the Legacy Leaders Academy. If you're a parent, sibling, friend, colleague, or student in some capacity, I will venture to guess that you're already playing the role of a leader in at least one particular area.

And well as far as the word expert goes, please recognize that EXPERT is an acronym that stands for education, experience, problem solver, execution, relevant to pain, and taking action. The key to becoming a standout authority as both an expert and a leader is by first choosing to focus on learning and sharing everything you can within one particular area of interest, ideally choosing a niche that's an inch wide and miles deep.

As individuals, when our curiosity peaks and we desire to have certain information on specific topics of interest, we'll seek out experts. We could choose to sort and sift through thousands of blog articles, pdf resources, and watch hours of how-to videos, but who has the time? When we want answers to our problems, we want them now. And most of us are willing to pay top-dollar for the proven short-cut solution.

Therefore it's no surprise that there's a significant demand for online coaching. When you step up as a leader in your field, there is no need for your clients to struggle through the pain and frustration you once did to learn what it is you know now. Instead, you can organize your knowledge with a little focus and get paid to share the solutions.

This world operates by a series of Universal laws, one of which states that everything (and everyone) is looking to take the shortest, quickest route at any given time. Your clients operate precisely the same way, and they will have no problem paying you for answers that will net them fast results.

Because of this inherent nature, we have ingrained within us humans; there will continue to be a high demand for coaching. The online space is continually evolving. You can become part of the online market evolution by starting your own coaching business today. This book will give you an overview of smart ways to establish income streams and what to look for in terms of opportunities and potential problems.

1

MONETIZE YOUR EXPERTISE

Choose a topic that piques your curiosity.

When it comes to identifying which area of expertise you should monetize, you'll want to choose an area of interest that you not only excel in, but that also currently piques your curiosity.

Because whether you realize it or not, you have many areas of expertise you could monetize. Might I suggest not selecting your focus-based area—of what you think will be profitable, but instead of something that strikes your curiosity. Otherwise, you could end up losing interest quickly, bringing the momentum boulder you worked tirelessly to tip your business into profits could come rolling back down the hill. You'll be back to square one with even less time, energy, and resources.

When I first got my start as a coach, I struggled with what to choose. At the time, I didn't think I was good at anything. It wasn't until a friend of mine encouraged me to sit down with a pen and paper and list everything I knew how to do. During this season of my life, professionally, I'd served eight years in the United States Army as a veterinary technician with a bachelor's degree in Biology. I was also working as a Certified Financial Advisor for a well-known bank. And I still didn't believe that I had any expertise worth monetizing.

I couldn't narrow down a niche, so I began to ask myself, "what are some questions that my friends and family ask me about all of the time and that I'm eager and excited to share the answers with them." A few things came to mind: animal care, finances, military tactics, and fitness. From there, I began to narrow down my choices by exploring which topics excited me.

Although I was working part-time at a local veterinary hospital, I no longer had a curiosity for veterinary medicine, so animal health care was off the table.

Occasionally I'd get questions about what it's like to handle a semi-automatic weapon. I knew how to assemble, disassemble, and fire an M-16, which I enjoyed, but again I had no interest in delving further into the arms world. Cross it off the list.

And finally, my ah-ha moment. I was an avid runner at the time, and often my co-workers would ask me questions about how to lose weight and get in shape. If I didn't know the answer on the spot, I was always buying the latest fitness magazine or searching for answers on the internet. Then I'd happily report back to them. Ding, ding, ding, I found my thing.

My ever-growing curiosity to expand my knowledge on health and fitness was my ticket to the coaching world and becoming boss. I slowly began building my coaching business, starting by helping my military friends get in shape for their upcoming mandatory physical fitness tests. Despite my 16 years of sports background, a bachelor's degree in Biology, becoming a Certified Strength & Conditioning Coach and pursuing my Master's Degree in Sports and Health Science. I lacked the confidence to see myself as an expert and leader. And way undercharged for my services initially.

Dumb, don't do this!

Finally, after strengthening my inner confidence muscle, I began to get serious about my business. I successfully took my newly launched coaching business from $0 to 6-figures in just under 6-months.

My initial business model was strictly me trading my time for money, which quickly lead to physical and then financial burnout—more on how to avoid this later.

Your ah-ha moment

If, for some reason, after putting in some careful thought, you're struggling to land on that one thing that will guarantee a successful coaching business, take a step back. Call upon three of your closest friends and ask them what they think your monetizable expertise should be. Too often, the thing that people will pay you most to help them with, you tend to take for granted because it comes easily or naturally to you. I challenge you not to disregard a topic because it feels too easy or fun. Instead, double down on it and allow yourself to move from a place of ease. Whoever told you that you must stress and struggle to earn money was seriously misinformed. Earning money can and should be fun and easy.

The bottom line, you have many areas of expertise that you could capitalize one, but you only need to choose one. Get started by choosing something that you're currently curious about so that as you continue to explore the topic and learn new information, you can quickly and enthusiastically share it with others—mostly getting paid to learn and grow as you go.

Earn as You Learn

University professors dedicate their lives to studying a particular subject matter and then show up to lecture to young, eager college students. They get paid to learn and teach. Wouldn't it be great if you could do the same?

Imagine being able to walk away from your 9 to 5 gig and double your income by studying an area you're interested in and sharing your finding with others. That's precisely the opportunity you're giving yourself when you step up and become an online coach.

Why coaching is a profitable endeavor

Humans, as an overall species, are lazy. We have no desire to chase down the in's and outs of any one particular problem. If we did, we'd have time for nothing else, and that's no way to live. So, when a specific issue does arise, we typically want it solved NOW.

When a problem arises, this is where your expertise comes in. Because you have a natural curiosity around that particular area of knowledge and willing to do the in-depth research around it, people will happily pay you for providing the answers.

Think of it this way. If you were experiencing signs and symptoms of a heart attack, wouldn't you rather pay top-dollar to see a cardiothoracic specialist vs. going to your local family doctor who may tell you to pop an aspirin and take a nap? The decision to invest in expert advice could mean the difference between life and death, literally.

The problem that you help other people solve doesn't have to be so dire for you to get paid to help them. For example, let's say that you're looking to lose the extra belly fat. You can rack your brain trying to go through all sorts of online forums and articles and watch endless amounts of irrelevant videos, leaving you in a cul-de-sac of confusion. Or you can go to somebody who knows their stuff and has solved the same problem that you're currently having in your own life.

After typing into your internet search bar "How to Lose Stubborn Belly Fat," a video link pops up and meets a friendly face that provides you with a quick answer to your question, and instantly you feel like you can trust them as an expert. At the end of the video, she asks you to visit her website and invites you to get a copy of her book. You read the book, finding it very informative, but you're hungry to learn more. An invitation to explore the expert's online course pings your inbox with the promise of melt away the belly fat without breaking into a sweat or giving up your favorite nightly sweet treat. You're in!

If you're like most people, you'd prefer to get the answers to your problems from an established expert than waste countless hours scouring the internet. You're even willing to pay for fast-track results. What's great about this is that if you tend to think this way, so will your ideal clients.

Here's the thing that I wish I'd understood early on in my coaching career. It is that even though people can find all of the answers to their problems for free on the internet, chances are they are just too busy to do the research. Or let's say that maybe they've done a little digging on their end, but since this subject matter is a reasonably new concept, they may feel inferior or unsure to implement their findings appropriately.

Whatever the case may be, your prospective clients would prefer to go to someone (like you) who simplifies the process and turns a problem into bite-sized actionable steps that help to solve their problem pronto.

It pays to be the boss.

Not everyone can be a boss. A certain level of self-confidence and self-discipline is required to be able to do so. But the fact that you're here right now tells me that you have some of the foundational pieces necessary to thrive as an entrepreneur.

How do I know this? Well, you're still reading, aren't you? Most people would get this book and never even crack the cover, but you aren't like most people, are you?

Good.

Now let's take a look at the employee mentality versus the entrepreneur mentality.

Employees: a good employee shows up to work and clocks in on time, does her job and punches out.

Most employees don't spend much time thinking about their job outside of work. They're there to do just enough to stay on the payroll, which keeps them caught in living the paycheck to paycheck life aka (j.o.b.) just over broke.

Entrepreneurs: financially successful entrepreneurs work all the time. Entrepreneurs work when they work, and they think about work when they're not 'working.'

Why? Because happy, successful entrepreneurs tend to choose an area of work that lights them up. Choosing work that doesn't feel like work; it feels fun.

But let's say that you're different, your above average, you tend to be world-class top-notch employee type who doesn't just show to the job to the bare minimum, collect your paycheck and roll out. Nope, you've taken a vested interest in the company that signs your paychecks.

Let's say you're the type of person who tends to go the extra mile—showing up early for work, staying late, taking additional courses, and acquiring promotion worthy certification after certification.

That's all well and good. I do not doubt that you bring a load of value to the company. The executives might even view you as irreplaceable and are incredibly grateful to have you on the payroll.

But, regardless of your work ethic, you're still just an employee with set wage-earning parameters. Even if you were eligible for a pay bump, your bonus depends its overhead vs. profit margins. Your boss could love you so much that they'd be thrilled to double or triple your salary, but unfortunately, it's not in the cards. So, you've hit an earning ceiling.

And let's not even talk about what if that company goes belly up. If you're not an active part of the company's quarterly financial decision-making process, then you can never be sure that you have job security, now can you?

When you choose to see yourself as an entrepreneur (yes, even if you still work for another company, it is possible to do both), your ability to exponentially increase your income lies entirely on your shoulders. You get to set your wage perimeters, work schedule, the requirements for whom you work with, and the capacity you work with them.

And when you choose to leverage your expertise by implementing intelligent online marketing strategies that set you up to receive passive income streams, a few are mentioned in this book; you bust through your potential earning ceiling, shatter it. You can now work half the time for double the amount of pay. Now add excellent customer service experience to the mix, and people begin to take notice.

The more you work on building your own thing outside of your 9 to 5 gig, the more you'll increase your value within the company who signs your paychecks. One outstanding recommendation leads to a new referral and then another. Before you know it, you've built yourself a professional brand that has skyrocketed beyond your wildest dreams.

Don't be surprised if people start pinging your inbox or blowing up your phone clamoring to interview you for their next blog article or podcast episode.

Get Paid to Answer People's Questions

One of the most rewarding areas of life is the opportunity to help other people thrive. Zig Ziglar said it best, "You can have everything in life you want if you just help enough other people get what they want."

When you can challenge the way a person has always done something, in such a way that it improves their life, it's one of the most rewarding experiences for both them and you.

Think about your own life; when someone shares a new and improved way of doing something with you that enhances your experience, however small it may seem; it creates a strong feeling of satisfaction, doesn't it? Clicking the puzzle pieces of problems together is a very positive experience for all parties involved.

When it comes to coaching, your clients will ask questions, and it's your job to share your answers. In exchange for these answers, you, the coach, are compensated with money. You're getting paid to sharpen your skills, knowledge, and expertise within your chosen subject matter. While simultaneously helping ease another's pain. It's a win-win all around!

Benefit from Passive Income Stream Models

Helping other people solve problems directly is cool, but what's even cooler is providing the answer once and getting paid again and again on automatic. When you choose to work in only the one-to-one model, you quickly cap out in earning potential. With only 24-hours in a day, and only so much a person is willing to pay you per hour.

Only trading your time for money is a severe problem because, first of all, there's only one of you, which means you're limited to the number of people you can serve. Unfortunately, technology hasn't provided us with the luxury of being able to be in two places at once.

Of the many coaches I've worked with thus far, it's no surprise that they come to me for help after trying their hand at the one-to-one model. This method alone quickly leads to overwhelm for them, much like I experienced when I first got started. And as rewarding as it is to help others achieve incredible results intimately, it also is the fastest way to burnout.

Active income is when you choose to trade your time for money, which means you earn it when you work. When you stop working, you stop receiving compensation. However, when you understand how to leverage your time with intelligent online tools, you can begin earning passive income—diligently working once to initially build an asset that you can later turn into an electronic money-making machine.

One of the best passive income assets you can build includes books. You work diligently initially to birth the book, and once it's published, if marketed correctly, it has the potential to generate profit for your business many times over.

In the brick and mortar world, an example of a passive income is buying real estate. You work to earn money to be able to buy the property. Outside of the occasional maintenance requirements, you just sit back and wait for the monthly lease money to hit your bank account. That is the power of passive income.

When you sell your expertise through passive assets, the good news is that you don't have to be coaching people face-to-face to earn your living. While I love direct coaching and do think that on some level you should consider adding it to your business model because it can be highly lucrative and rewarding, I do not believe that it should be your only stream of revenue. You need to establish passive streams of income as well, and how to do that is what I'm going to break down for you step-by-step in this book. Take a deep breath, your days of just trading your time for money are nearly over.

I'll give you a brief overview of a few potential passive income streams you can establish in your own coaching business in the next chapter. Then we'll dive more deeply into the how-to's of each in upcoming sections.

2

ONLINE INCOME STREAMS

This chapter will provide you with a quick overview of how you can create online income streams by selling your expertise. Once you've decided to step up and become an online coach, please note that there are many ways to earn a handsome income. And not every option will be the best for you. This chapter intends to provide you with an overview of a few proven money-generating strategies. I'm going to devote the following sections for each of these specific methods.

Sell books

Building a powerful professional brand is how real experts cultivate authority. They start with books. They write down what they know on a specific topic in books. When enough books on your area of expertise become publicized, it won't be long until people begin asking you to speak at seminars and be lining up around the block wanting to work with you one-on-one.

Whether you love writing or don't, once you publish a book, you're perceived as an expert because most people are too intimidated by the thought of writing a book that they never do it. By simply organizing your knowledge into an outline, writing down your thoughts on the subject, sharing a few stories that help drive home the point you make, and publishing your work, you've stepped into the professional world's upper ranks.

Becoming a published author, even when you self-publish, means several things.

First, you have to have something worth sharing. Maybe it's an exciting story. Perhaps it's some sort of expertise or inside knowledge.

Secondly, you are a disciplined person to see a project through. If you can do that, your clients will have more faith in you that you'll see their coaching session through as well.

Finally, you are resourceful. You're the type of person who can take something that seems complicated to another person and streamline inside one written asset.

Regardless of the personal stance of self-publishing, when you write and sell books, other people will grant you instant authority and because they know how hard it is to organize one's thoughts.

When you publish books, you allow more people to buy your books, aka your expertise. The more people who become aware of you and your offerings, the stronger your brand becomes. The healthier your brand becomes, the more money you earn.

It's a continuous cycle that just keeps on giving. In other words, your business's value grows by merely doing you and sharing your answers. And if you want to build a red hot audience of raving fans, you simply let more people know about who you are and what solutions you offer. It's that straight forward.

Building your audience can be done through new content creation, media production, interviews, guest blogging, and articles, just to name a few. The more you share your answers with others, the more powerful your brand becomes. Compare this with working for somebody else.

Video courses

When it comes to selling your expertise, one of my most favorite mediums is videos. Videos can be shot quickly and cheaply from your smartphone. You can pre-record them and invite people to pay you to view them. Charging people to see your videos can be done as a one-off offer or an ongoing event inside a membership vault. Coaching this way is considered passive income because you work diligently once to create the video content but then have the capacity to earn money from them many times over.

One of the most effective ways to teach someone something new isn't by having them just read something you wrote. Nope. A more effective way of teaching calls for incorporating auditory, visual, and tactile experiences. To teach effectively, this is where video creation becomes your friend.

When people are watching a video of you speaking directly to them, they pay close attention to your eyes, facial expressions, and body language.

Much of what you are saying comes through in what you don't say. The camera hides nothing. Using video can be intimidating for many, but when you are sharing from an authentic, helpful place, video can be one of the fastest ways to build rapport, this is important because people are more likely to buy from those they know, like and trust.

Video courses work because when people watch you, they can see your enthusiasm for the topic. That enthusiasm is contagious, which invites the viewer to absorb the information that is shared while simultaneously building up your authority, credibility, and desire to reciprocate what you've given them by buying your products or services.

Webinars

Hosting webinars is a great way to establish a stream of passive income. They're like in-person seminars, only done online via a video conferencing tool. You can have your prospective clients fill out a form and pay a fee to access your teachings.

Your webinars can be held live or pre-recorded and scheduled to present on automatic. If set up correctly, your clients go through an automated sales funnel that will allow them to select a day and time to attend the webinar that best works. They receive automatic prompts that remind them to show up and watch the presentation. There are many pros and cons to using this method, more on this in an upcoming chapter.

When you conduct a live webinar, it's great to open the conversation to the viewer by asking them to follow up questions either as you present the lesson or after. A pro tip always be sure to record so that you can resell the training at another time if you so choose. No matter which type of webinar you decide to host, they typically run no more than 2-hours, focusing on a relatively narrow range of topics

Keep in mind that even if you're presenting the same core lessons, different audiences have different interests and questions. And when selecting the time and date to offer, be sure first to check the social climate. You may not want to schedule your webinars around major holidays or events. Doing so might significantly decrease your show up and sales rates.

VIP One-to-One Coaching

There is no higher version of personalized service you could offer than by having VIP packages where you work with only one client at a time. This form of coaching is terrific because you're able to get to the heart of the matter with your clients and genuinely offer personalized advice and strategies to help them have a life-altering transformation. And you can charge premium rates for premium service. However, there are a few drawbacks to this business model.

Automatic. This revenue channel is still considered an active income. Meaning that you MUST show up, do the work in real-time to receive payment.

While there are elements of the VIP customer journey experience that you can automate, such as inviting your prospective client to visit your website, fill out a form, auto-book a coaching call with you, and send follow-up emails and notifications of

It's a great option to add to your business model mix, especially if you're just starting, but I'd warn again, making it your only revenue stream because it can quickly lead to burnout.

Your Business Model Mix

When it comes to building your business model money streams, there's no right or wrong mix. Each coach will feel more drawn to one type vs. the other. However, if you are serious about building a rock-solid, a reliable offer expert brand, you might want to consider doing all five because if you think about it, they all grow into the next.

The bullet points you use to outline your book you use as inspiration for blog articles. The blog articles can become video scripts that you can use for a marketing lead magnet to attract new prospective clients or sold as a course. Those video series could be linked together to create pre-scheduled webinars that you could use to vet your potential VIP clients. Bundle your video into a class. And your live webinar skills could also be used to teach your clients either in a 1:1 setting or as a small group coach

Building opportunity.

Here's the thing, the more content you publish, the more credibility and authority your professional brand will gain. The more influence and credibility your brand gains, the more opportunity for new people to learn about your brand, and the more your prospective clients' list will grow. The larger your list becomes, the higher your chances of converting them into clients, i.e., money in the bank for your business.

In my opinion, it all begins with your book. If people like your book, they'll be more likely to register for your webinar. Then they may want to pay for your video courses or your one-to-one coaching packages. Each of these different channels reinforces you to them. They don't necessarily cancel each other out.

As you continue to show up and serve others, word will spread like wildfire about your ability to solve that annoying problem people have. Some people will be content with your passive service streams, and others will be asking you to provide one-on-one coaching for them.

It is allowing you to conduct your coaching sessions in person or online. You can do this on a variety of video conferencing platforms; it doesn't matter. What matters most to people, if your ability to help solve their problem.

Depending on your unique area of expertise, you might be able to command hundreds of dollars per coaching hour. Top earners tend to charge quite a bit of money coaching people online, and it all boils down to developing a trustworthy personal brand.

3

BRANDING YOU

When it comes to building a brand, there is no more unique option to brand than to brand you. You are unique and wonderfully made. You have a point of view, unlike anyone else. And guess what people not only want to know about it, and they're willing to pay you for it!

An excellent way to get paid to share your point of view while giving your brand the mega-boost it needs is through writing and publishing books. It shows people dedication to your work and helps to set you up as a professional.

You're someone with something to say and worth listening to all because you've taken the initiative to organize your thoughts into a book.

Publishing books, even short ones, is a fantastic way to advertise your expertise and help prime your prospective clients into working with you more closely. To set yourself apart as a coach, I recommend that you start by focusing on solving ONE problem at a time. Begin by learning all you can about that one area of focus and write your first book.

There's no need to be the go-to expert on every micro-subject with your area of expertise; if done, your brand may just be white noise. To build a truly memorable brand, and stay top of mind to your ideal clientele, focus your first book or series of books on one specific sub-niche within your niche.

Covering cardio, strength training, macro calculating, and micronutrition, maybe just get started by focusing on self-love or a paper on simple substitutions so you can feel great without feeling deprived.

Focus will help you stand out as a go-to expert, but it will also help your perfect clients find you.

For example, let's pretend that you're a personal trainer who wants to help women gain body confidence and learn how to have a healthy relationship with food. Instead of writing a book

Attempting to publish a book that claims to answers everything about your industry simply won't sell. Choose to answer only 1 or 2 questions within your book, then narrow in on the critical points within that sub-niche. Narrowing your

Think of your book as your business card. It's an opportunity to share your story, tell the world who you are, and help. People don't need to know everything you know to see you as the expert that you are. They only need to read what you have to say on any one specific topic, to show them that you walk the talk.

Advantages of coaching through books

A few primary advantages of writing and publishing a book are that it gives you instant credibility, and it's an easy way to set up your first stream of passive income. You do the work once, or maybe even hire out a ghostwriter (yes, you can do that), and then it becomes an asset that you can sell again and again on automatic, generating your income for years to come.

Many published authors make thousands of dollars off of a book that they'd written several years before. They only worked once to publish it, but every single year, the money rolls in. You can do the same with your books. And this is true whether there distributed through traditional methods or self-publishing channels.

Become an author instantly sets you apart from your peers. We'd be silly not to address the fact that there are many experts in the same specialization as you. However, not all of them can (or are willing to) write a book. Perhaps it's because they don't have the time or the discipline to do it. But like we previously discovered, you are different. You have a book idea, and you're willing to bring it to life. Your willingness to organize your thoughts for the benefit of others gives you a tremendous competitive advantage.

A lot of expert coaches get their start by self-publishing. They make quite a bit of money and are recognized experts in their field. Later on their offered traditional publishing deals, and often the work they self-published gets revisions and re-released under the publishing house. You can do the same. The key here is to permit yourself to become a published author first, don't wait around for a book deal.

Now to truly maximize your author brand, you'll want to be sure to direct your readers back to your primary website. Think of your website as your storefront. Instead of (or as an extension to) your brick and mortar building where you traditionally invite prospective clients to visit, use your website. Your website is a place to highlight your expertise status as well as directly share more information with people as to how you can help them. When people click on your website, they see your picture, biography, resume, and other experiences. In other words, they get the information they need to determine whether you are the go-to expert for them or not.

Secondly, it shows your readers that you're more than an author. They're on your website. Your beloved readers will have the opportunity to discover how else they can learn from you, whether by registering for an upcoming webinar, enrolling in your digital courses or working with you one-on-one. You've not only successfully attracted ideal prospective clients, but now you have the perfect opportunity to convert them into paying clients.

Not a great writer?

The good news here is you can do quick work of developing a reliable brand through book publishing in your area of expertise without having to write a single sentence. How? Outsourcing.

Honestly, you don't have to lift a finger to write the material that you publish. You can easily hire low cost, high volume, high-quality writing services through one of the many virtual writing platforms available.

Your hired ghostwriter, who loves writing, will crank out book after book for you and sign your name for it. You'll want to proofread the text and be sure to add your own 'isms' to it so that it's adequately reflected in your voice. But that's the easy and fun part! Leave the hard part to someone else who doesn't think it's all that hard because it's their zone of genius.

All you need to do is select the topic you want to discuss and outline the key bullet points. Perhaps even provide a few stories of your own that help to make your point. You can do this by using the audio recorder on your phone and speak into it directly and then simply forward the file to your writer. Easy! Doing this will allow you to publish more books more quickly.

And the more books you publish, the more of an expert you become. Now I won't lie, at first you'll need to put forth the effort to promote your books. But once you've gained a solid fan base, the more books you publish, the less you'll need to improve. Why? Your older books will have promoted your website so much that when people join your mailing list, you only need to send out an update or two to tell people that your latest book has arrived to rack up sales.

Disadvantages

A word of warning! Publishing a book doesn't necessarily lead to big sales, especially if you're just starting. Although books are a form of passive income, if you're just starting your coaching career and no one has heard of you, you'll need to do a significant amount of marketing before you experience financial gain.

First, I'd like you to see your book as your business card, maybe even something that you give away for free as your building your brand so that people can more easily discover who you are and how you can help them.

At the beginning of your career, please plan to spend time, effort, and yes, even money, to promote your books. Publishing your book is not one of those fields of dream moments, "build it, and they will come." Unfortunately, it doesn't work that way. But over time, as more and more people learn about you, your books can and will become an automatic passive income stream for your business.

I just want you to keep this in mind, this is not something that will happen overnight, and that's ok. True leaders rise to the top after logging in countless hours of unpaid work consistently. If you want to become a standout authority in your area of expertise, you'll need to do the same.

Step by step guide

Step 1: Focus on a niche

When you first begin to build your professional brand, it's easy to get shiny object syndrome and want to build out several elements to your business at once—word of advice: focus solely on one niche. Decide which type of people you want to help most and how you'll help them. Then dedicate yourself to become a master on that one topic. When selecting your first niche to focus on, choose one that's an inch wide but a mile deep, meaning that you want to serve a targeted area with high demand.

For example, you could offer expert advice on underwater basket weaving. No doubt, this is a specific niche, but are there enough people out there willing to read a book on the subject, much less want to sign up for VIP coaching for it? If the answer is no, you won't earn enough money to make it worth your time. Perhaps you select another topic.

Step 2: Leverage Amazon

To help you determine if the topic you've selected to focus on is a viable, money earning topic, look no further than Amazon. Head to their bookstore and do a quick category search on their site.

Pay attention to the sales ranking within your particular niche. If the top seller lists have ten thousand sales or lower, chances are you've selected a high demand niche.

Step 3: Select your sub-niche

Once you've found an area to focus on, I want to challenge you to drill down and select a sub-niche within that niche. Use a helpful tool like KDSPY to help you find ideal keyword demand patterns on Amazon. Conduct a keyword search to seek out books published on similar topics, then determine what theme you can write on to bring something fresh to the market space.

Step 4: Outline, Produce and Publish Your Book

Now that you have your ideal topic selected with your sub-niche category, sit down, and bullet points out the first answers you'll provide within your book.

Next, write the book. Or record your thoughts and outsource the writing to a virtual ghostwriter. Consider using a helpful tool like Grammarly to ensure that your spelling and punctuation are correct. For an additional fee, Grammarly will also compare your written content to other works published online to ensure that it's 100% original and not at all plagiarized. You can also hire a publisher if you so chose.

When it comes time to publish your final work, there are many options out there; my suggestion is to use Kindle Direct Publishing. It's relatively straight-forward. Their website offers how-to videos as well as templates, but this is also something we do together step-by-step inside of my coaching experience, The Income Amplifier.

Step 5: Link it

Within every book that you publish, be sure to add a link to your primary website. This official website is not just your online calling card; it's not just a place to put a beautiful image. Nope, it's a place to provide easy to follow next-step 'arrows' to the action you wish your readers to take next. It's an opportunity to invite the reader further to buy one of your other products or services.

Step 6: Identify your next book topic

Now that you've diligently identified the area of expertise, you'll focus on first and drilled down into a specific sub-niche to leverage to carve out a place for your professional brand to shine, it's time to take a look and which topics you could cover next. You might consider taking the conversation of book one a little further by slightly pivoting into a few key questions not answered in book one, but that would make sense to answer in book two.

Step 7: Repeat the process

Continue to write book after book within your area of expertise. The more books you write and publish on any one specific area, the faster you'll build brand awareness, authority, and a red-hot audience eager and excited to work you.

4

BUSINESS MODELS THAT WORK

There are several business models for coaches out there, my favorite? Digital course creation using video, much like I do inside of the Legacy Leaders Academy.

With this particular approach, you're going to identify and solve a core problem using a series of videos. Ensuring that your thoughts are well organized and that your videos are concise. I recommend that you write out your video scripts ahead of time, and make sure that each scenario covers a specific topic before recording. When your clients view your videos in totality, they will get the information that they wanted to learn. You can then present your video course through a designated membership access area in which you can then charge them a one-time payment or a monthly recurring fee.

Advantages

The significant advantage of selling video courses is that you get a passive income business. You spend some time upfront to initially create the digital asset, but then can sell it again and again, ideally on automatic so that there is no limit to the number of people you can serve at any given time.

Another critical advantage of video courses is that you can use your book content as inspiration for your class. Showing up on camera creates a more personalized experience for your clients.

Reading books is great, but let's be honest. It requires quiet, focused time to digest. A book is written in black and white and requires the reader to use their imagination to paint a picture in their mind, whereas a video course can help convey the concepts more clearly in a shorter amount of time.

Video is the fastest way to build your brand's KLT Factor (know, like trust) for your audience. When you look straight into the camera, people can connect with you on a more intimate level. And the best part? They feel connected to you, even without you being physically there.

Video helps to show the viewer that you're human and that you have an emotional range. Your voice and body language say a lot more than just the words coming out of your mouth.

Often books alone can limit your ability to express your point of view truly. But the video, even if you tend to be a little camera shy, helps to convey your message more powerfully.

Disadvantages

I'd be lying if I didn't address the fact that sometimes coaching through video has its disadvantages. While for some people (especially introverts) who relish in the ability to control their environment and be able to connect with hundreds or thousands of people from across the globe from the comfort of their own home, there is a slight downside to this. While the viewers beyond the lens can get a good understanding of who you are and can connect with you on an intimate level, you as the content creator may become disconnected since there isn't a direct way for you to connect back with them.

One of the hardest things we humans have to do daily is to communicate our point of view to another accurately. Without immediate feedback, there's a chance that your letter has been misinterpreted and not adequately received.

As experts, we're often too close to our work that it can be easy to leave out critical elements of information. Despite your best efforts, if you don't have a channel to receive viewer feedback, you can successfully cover a good 90% of the details of the topic at hand, but what about the other 10%? Therefore teaching your courses live before turning them into an evergreen option is a smart way to go.

Step-by-step guide

Step #1 Market on Your Corner

Avoid competition as much as possible. Have a look at your industry and decide who your direct competitors are. Your chosen topic must be well-covered. Then decide to make a slight pivot and stake your flag in a sub-topic that provides answers for your ideal clients.

A great way to do this is to identify your personal brand story. Ask yourself why you're interested in becoming a coach within your chosen subject matter. Then decide who exactly you'd like to help and how you'd like to help them.

There's no need to show up to a crowded 'corner' and try to outsell brands that have staked their claim long before your arrival. Take a look at what they're doing, alter your approach slightly, and market on a different street corner.

Step #2 Identify Your U.S.P.

Identify your U.S.P. (unique selling proposition), i.e., what sets you apart. To get started, take a look at what your competitors are already doing first. Ask yourself, "How do they show up in the marketing place? What problems do they solve? How do they describe their brand?" What area of service do they not cover, and are you willing to fill in the 'holes' for your clients?

Then I want you to notice the words they use to market their business. What types of headlines do they use? What kind of stories do they tell or content do they publish? How can you come up with something better that might entice others to share?

If marketing isn't your strength, don't stress. Please note that it is a learnable skillset if you so desire to put in the work. Or you could hire a marketing coach, like myself, who can help bubble up the answers within you to the surface.

Step #3 Write Your Sales Script

When it comes time to publish your work, there are many easy-to-use platforms out there that require little to no tech-skill. You simply create an account, upload your course content, type in a few extra prompted details, and publish it. Voila, you have an online course!

Now, you could leave it and go on about your business, hoping that people find your course amongst thousands hosted on that particular site. Or you could take it one step further and create a custom sales video to add to your sales page.

My advice? Take the time to make the video. Please do not waste this opportunity.

These days most people have multiple devices in front of them at once. You have only a few seconds to grab their attention and to tell them why they should register for your course now, so don't leave it up to your written words to do the job.

Work with a mentor who can teach you the in's and out's of how-to-write a phenomenal sales video script. Then take the time to record, edit, and upload it to your course sales page platform. You want to be able to get your message across loud and clear. And adding a little fun to your video doesn't hurt either. Remember, if you're having fun, the viewer will have fun too.

Step #4 Under-promise and Over-deliver

If you are offering coaching in any subject area with decent demand levels, don't be surprised if many people are providing the same information. How do you stand out? How do you win over your prospective client?

It's simple: under-promise and over-deliver. When people register for your offering, give them so much value that they can't help but tell their friends. Go the extra mile and provide an unexpected next-step bonus that will more than set them up for success.

Step #5 Use worksheets to up-sell your offer

You can easily add extra value by creating a few supplementary support PDF materials such as worksheets, cheat sheets, templates, or swipe files that your clients can easily download.

These bonus items could be linked inside of your book to entice your readers to take the next step into buying a seat to your upcoming webinar or video course. Or they could be used on the backend as an up-sell option when they purchase another product.

Regardless of how you use them, you'll want to ensure that they provide value to the user. A generic worksheet won't cut it. Remember that you are in charge of your brand and every published piece, pdf worksheet, article, book, or otherwise needs to reflect your brand accurately and what it is you stand for.

If you don't consider yourself all that tech-savvy, or perhaps you simply don't have the time to create extra support materials. You can outsource items for as little as $5/hour.

Use your worksheets to build up your brand and close sales. At the very least, within the sheets, invite people to share the word about you and your offering.

Step #6 Create a digital hub to house all the content you create

Chances are if people have found your work and love your work, they'll be looking for more, make it easy for them to see by creating a digital hub to house all the content you create.

For example, if your expertise is winemaking. You can start by creating content on how to make one type of wine. After that, you can focus on another sub-niche like sparkling wine. Make content on that. Then after that, use dry wines or something else.

By the time you've completed, you should've covered all the sub-niches involved with wine. Do this, regardless of the niche you choose. Maybe you're into drawing, crafting, or design. Whatever the case may be, hone in on the sub-niches by using the steps previously mentioned.

Those who are interested in what you're interested in will find you. Because chances are, if you're typing questions into the search bar about it, your perfect ideal customers are too. And the more content you publish, the more your name will come up again and again, and they'll start to create an association between your brand and that particular field of expertise.

5

WEBINARS

Hosting webinars (online seminars) is a fun and low-cost way to get your name out and build your brand as an online coach. Whether you conduct them live or pre-schedule a video recording, they are a great way to leverage your time by sharing them with many people at once.

Your attendees can register for the presentation in advance, and if you so choose, you can ask them to select an ideal time and date that works best for them. As the coach, you outline your talking points or perhaps put together a slide presentation, and you present the information to your online audience.

To set up your webinar on automatic so that it can run multiple times a day. The content that you share within the presentation needs to be evergreen, meaning that it can withstand the test of time.

Putting together a useful evergreen webinar takes time and effort, but they are worth getting right. Because once you have them correctly set up, they could be generating you money automatically so that you can hit up happy hour with your girlfriends instead of sitting at your desk, biting your nails to the nub, wondering how or when you're next client will come in.

Advantages

You can choose to set up your webinar to run on a free or fee basis. They are a great way to build brand awareness, provide high-value to your clients in a small amount of time while simultaneously growing your email list.

There are many incredible webinar platforms out there that you can use to set up automatic data collection, email reminders, and follow up support to attendees quickly.

By creating specific time slots for viewing the webinar, you create a perceived sense of scarcity that encourages your attendees to take action and to show up for your presentation. It's then up to you to push yourself to present your best materials in terms of graphics and concise content so that your attendees can experience a mico-transformation within your 1-2-hour presentation.

Webinars can be used as a part of your overall promotional campaigns or as a passive stream of income. Pull your lesson together, record it once, and you can get paid many times over.

Disadvantages

One key disadvantage of using this form of coaching is that it has a potential lack of engagement. Your pre-recorded evergreen webinar presentation shows you talking to the camera with no direct way for your viewers to engage with you in real-time.

Because you have shot this material ahead of time and are focusing on a relatively narrow topic, you might be teaching things that aren't interesting to the viewer or potentially glaze over, mentioned in passing, or not fully explored. Talk about a let-down. You could bet that people will feel doubly disappointed if they had paid to view the presentation, which could considerably undermine your brand.

Step-by-step guide

To use webinars as a way to sell your coaching services, you need to do the following:

Step #1 Pick a webinar hosting platform

There are many excellent webinar hosting platforms that you can choose. When narrowing down your search, consider one that offers in-payment collection and an additional 'easy share' button for social promotions.

It's beneficial to have an easy way to encourage your registrants to share the webinar with their inner circles on social media.

Step #2 Write your video script

Spend some time crafting your message. Remember that you are an expert on the topic you're about to share. Your audience isn't. There's no need to overwhelm them, keep in mind that less is more. And do your best to share the information in easy to digest bite-sized tidbits.

Step #3 Shoot your video

Feeling totally at ease on camera doesn't come naturally for anyone, it takes practice, so don't stress. Do your best to relax, smile, and make eye contact with the camera lens.

Try your best to keep in mind that you are speaking to a real-life person as you record.

If you plan to make edits to your video, feel free to do a couple of takes. But remember progress over perfection. People have a hard time connecting with perfectly polished, so don't stress that you're not.

Also, it's ok to use a prop or two to help emphasize your point, but try not to make the entire video about any one object because it can quickly become distracting and take away from the information you're sharing.

Step #4 Do outreach and promote

Before anyone can buy into you, you must buy into yourself.

Repeat after me: "There is no shame in self-promotion."

Wouldn't it be oh so lovely if you could wake up, and people just instantly knew who you were and how you could help? Unfortunately, even the biggest stars and influencers all started outs as 'nobodies.'

I know that it can feel weird to promote yourself but do it anyway. If you genuinely know within your bones that your answers could help improve another person's life, you're robbing them of their transformation by not sharing your opportunity.

Promote. Promote. Promote.

Step #5 Set up your appointment scheduler

Within your webinar platform, you should be able to locate the appointment scheduler tool quickly. Be sure to select a few dates and times that you're willing to run the training video so that your clients can choose which days and times work best.

There's no right or wrong answer here, but as a general rule of thumb for evergreen webinars, I like to set one option to start 15 minutes after they've clicked on the landing page because at that moment there in the zone, hungry for answers and eager to learn. So why not 'strike' while the iron is hot?!

The 15-minute window is just enough time for them to build anticipation for what's to come, use the restroom, grab a snack, pen, and paper, and settle in before the presentation. But not so long that they'll busy themselves with something else. Make sense?

Again there's no right or wrong answer here, so feel free to experiment with different time frames for your webinars.

Step #6 Set up an email marketing system

One of the great things about automation platforms like a webinar hosting is that many of them come with automated email marketing campaigns that you can easily customize and turn on to send autoresponders to your attendees before and promptly after the training session. Be sure to set yours up!

6

LIVE TRAINING

Live webinars involve presenting an actual live presentation in front of an audience in real-time. For this presentation, it's best to keep the topic narrow and to answer a few questions.

Since you'll have a live audience in attendance, it's best to ask them questions throughout the presentation. You can have them type their answers in the side chatbox, or bring them into the conversation via audio and video.

Typically your plan to host your live webinar as a one-time event that you pre-schedule for one particular day and time.

When your attendees join you live, it's always nice to get their direct feedback by allowing for a follow-up Q&A session at the end. Keep in mind that every audience will be a little different and will bring different questions to the table, even if you're presenting the same bullet points on a particular topic.

Do your best to answer their questions. If there is an answer that you don't know, avoid saying, "I don't know." Instead, be the leader that they seek, reassure them that that's an excellent question that you wish to investigate further and get back to them on it soon. If you do say this, be sure that you do just that. Investigate it further and then get back to them on it asap.

Advantages

Live webinars are a great way to deliver massive value to your audience, but it's also an excellent tool to use to grow your email list. Treat your email list like gold because well, it is.

These are not just names and emails that your collecting. There are real-life people, with real problems, with credit/debit cards who are willing to pay you to help them solve their problem.

Again, you can host your live webinars for free or for a fee. Don't be afraid to invite them to pay for your live training session. Because you're showing up in real-time to answer the different audiences' questions, they'll be willing to pay you for it. But be sure to bring your best materials forward so that you accurately highlight your expertise.

Disadvantages

You have to know your stuff. Don't bank on 'faking it til you make it.' If you don't know your thing, it'll show. Because you're showing up live, in real-time, the camera hides nothing.

It's ok to be a bit nervous about going live; people will give your grace because they too would shy to go live. But if you're going to be nervous, at least be sure that you know the in's and out's of the topic your about to share.

Also, be quick on your feet. As impressive as the call and response dynamic may be. It can also wreak havoc on your nerves. Stay alert and listen to each person's question fully. Repeat back to them what they've asked. Doing this ensures that you understood the problem, and it buys your brain a little time to formulate the answer. Then do your best to quickly and succinctly answer the question in full. Doing so will boost your brand power and set up to look like the pro you are.

Step-by-step guide

Step #1 Pick a live webinar software platform

At the very least, this platform must have a billing and promotional component. It must also have an email collection component or tie into your current email collection system for your mailing list. For my top platform picks, visit MollyAnnLuna.com/SmartTools.

Step #2 Pick a date

It's essential to pick the right strategic date. You don't want to choose a time that is too close because people might have made another plan. Be careful not to select a year so far that people will forget or worse find a coach who can help solve their problem more quickly. There has to be enough urgency in the period. Creating a sense of urgency will increase the likelihood that lots of people will book your live webinar.

Step #3 Practice

Bullet point your topic and practice running through your lesson. Prepare for any potential questions that you think might come up during the live call.

Show up knowing your thing. You don't want to look like a deer stuck in headlights. The work you've done to build your brand will go up in smoke if people don't think that you're on top of your game. Before going live, brush up on your bullet points. Then smile, relax, have fun, and share your answers.

Step #4 Be enthusiastic

Enthusiasm is contagious. If you show up eager and excited to discuss the topic at hand, so will your audience. Careful not to be overly enthusiastic, as that can be a turn off quickly. Use various voice inflections throughout the presentation to help emphasize multiple points.

Step #5 Remember that your brand reputation is at stake

Throughout the call, no matter if you have a tech glitch, a tongue twist, or an unexpected interruption, do your best to stay cool, calm, and in control. Mistakes happen, it's life. Your audience will forgive you. Do your best to remain professional throughout the presentation, and be careful not to insult any of your attendees. Take a deep breath, relax, and have fun.

Step #6 Ask people to take the next step

Even if this is a paid presentation, the chances are that your audience will want more. So be sure always to invite them to take the next steps, whether that be to buy your book, your video course, attend your next live session, or register to become a VIP client.

Remember that people showed up to your live event because they seek answers, support, and guidance. Be that guide for them, and always ask them to take the next step.

Don't be afraid to ask your attendees to share the 'next step' opportunity with their circle of influence. If people enjoy your content and find real value from it, they'll be excited to share it with their friends and friends.

MOLLY ANN LUNA

7

GETTING PAID TO COACH

Thus far in the book, we've primarily covered coaching opportunities that provide more passive streams of income, but I'd be remiss if we didn't' spend a little of time focusing on how to get paid to coach your clients in a one-to-one model directly.

This form of coaching is an active form of coaching. Meaning that you must fully show up for your client at the time of your scheduled booking and actively coach them in real-time.

Whatever questions or insecurities they may have, you're there to help them by providing customized solutions. You're operating on a more personal level, really getting to the heart of the issue.

As previously mentioned, I successfully built my first coaching business $0 to 6-figures in just under 6-months ONLY using this method, so it is a proven model and a potentially lucrative one. There are certain advantages as well as a few disadvantages that I'd like to highlight.

Advantages

The most apparent advantage of one-to-one coaching is that this is the most expensive form of coaching; this where you make the big bucks.

If you have developed a reliable brand in your area of expertise, you can charge hundreds of dollars per hour. Imagine earning $300 up to $500 an hour. Not too bad, right? Cut out the commute time and strictly offer coaching from your laptop, and you could potentially book back-to-back sessions, which will help you stack racks quickly.

Another key advantage is that since this style of coaching is personal and you customize the content to the ONE individual you're working with, there's potentially not a need to do a ton of pre-call prep work.

Disadvantages

Even if you have the qualifications and experience to be able to charge premium hourly rates from your previous career, you may be required to 'pay your dues' upfront when it comes to starting your coaching practice. When exposed to a new audience who's never heard of you before, you'll need to spend a significant amount of time building your professional brand and getting the word out about the transformation you can provide.

I wish I could tell you that you just pop up a VIP coaching landing page with a buy button and get booked out months in advance, but unfortunately, it's now how things work in the online coaching world.

Part of the reason for my quick coaching success was because I'd leverage my immediate network, a network that I'd spent years cultivating before. I then provided top-notch service and was able to build my business primarily off of referrals. But even then, I started my coaching business charging a measly $5 an hour and then bumped it up to $20, then $50, then $100, then $125, $145, and finally up to $500 an hour.

I had the credentials to back up my hourly rate, but I needed social proof to justify the prices for new clients to see the value.

Here's the thing; your name has to be prominent enough for people to say, "Yes. That person's time is worth $300 or more per hour." The value first starts in your mind and is proven via your continued action towards building your brand. That's how it works.

Another key disadvantage is that these one-to-one coaching sessions are costly in time, money, and energy. At the end of the day your selling your time for money. You can't be somewhere else, doing anything else, or helping any other people. You're locked in, coaching your one client for that one session. Yes, you're getting paid a lot of money per hour, but you're still trading your time for money. And that's time that could potentially be spending prospecting future clients.

Far too often, I see coaches get caught up in a feast or famous cycle. A season comes, and they're booked with VIP clients, coaching, earning, coaching, and earning. But once those contracts end, they're back to square one. Since all of their time was used to care for the clients in front of them, there was no extra time and space to attract and nurture new clients to the degree in which they sign on as VIPs, hence the feast or famous cycle.

And while I've seen coaching in this service phase, yes, they may be earning top-dollar for that time, but the key thing to remember when it comes to private, personalized coaching is that it's just that, individual. Generally speaking, you can't record your sessions or reuse any of that coaching content for future use. Reselling a one-to-one session is a big no-no. After all, your VIP client paid you to interact with them directly. They're not asking you to turn their experience into the content to make money repeatedly by selling their recorded session.

On a final note, you might have to produce custom worksheets for this one-to-one session. You are potentially taking up quite a bit of time. If that person has very specialized needs, this can take more effort than you have originally anticipated.

Creating customized plans is what I did in my first coaching business model. I provided customized fitness and nutrition plans. I'll be the first to admit that this element alone set my business up in flames. The workload becomes too overwhelming, and I, along with my company, burnt to the ground.

Therefore, I highly recommend that you don't model your coaching business on the one-to-one model alone. It's best to mix-and-max with a few passive income streams as well. That way, when you need to take a break so that you can mentally and emotionally reset, your business doesn't stop earning money.

For those of you who are interested in getting started with direct coaching here's your step-by-step guide:

Step-by-step guide

Step #1 Set up your appointment system

Directly on your website or by using landing page software, create an easy to find a page that lists the details of your coaching packages. To include the transformation you'll provide, the promise you'll deliver on, the price per session, your terms and conditions, refund policy, etc.

Then add an appointment button that allows your clients to book their session. If you're just starting, there are plenty of free options you can use to get started, such as Calendly, PickTime, or SetMore. For more robust features, you can upgrade to a paid plan. Set it up and then link it to your live one-on-one webpage.

Establishing your brand page is a lot easier than it sounds. Don't worry, I can show you how to do this step-by-step inside the Online Business Clinic Mentorship program.

Step #2 Add payment collection

Some 'plug and chug' website templates and landing page templates will easily allow you to be active in their payment integration tool. If, for some reason, the software you've chosen doesn't offer this feature, you can use an application such as Paypal for business or my favorite Stripe. It's free to use, and they only deduct a small processing service fee from each transaction.

Get paid upfront BEFORE you conduct the session. Overcome your fear of thinking, "If I ask for money, this person will walk away." Well, if they're going to walk away anyway because they're not sure, then they were never your customers, to begin. Do you see what I mean? Don't waste your time with lookie-loos.

Step #3 Review your clients' background materials before each session

Before your one-to-one session, spend some time reviewing your clients' background materials before each session is critical. You have to deliver substantial value. You're not just spouting the same stuff that you say to every random person in the street interested in your areas of expertise.

This person is asking for a one-to-one coaching session for a reason. They have specific needs and interests, so do your best to address each of them adequately.

Read up on these, do your research. Give your clients the information they don't already know. Break this information down so they can get value from the one-to-one coaching.

Step #4 Show up on time

Showing up on time, every time, and be professional. No excuses.

Step #5 Ask for the next booking

At the end of your call, take the initiative and ask for the next booking. That is, of course, if it's appropriate that you continue with more coaching sessions. The best time to get your client to commit to their transformation is while they're in it.

When it comes to building an online coaching business, there is no right or wrong way to do things; there's just a better way. And take it from someone like me who's helped thousands of online coaches get their start. While leveraging online tools to earn money is fantastic, digitals tools to keep your business in operation can add up quickly. To help you keep your business overhead low, I highly suggest that you kickstart your new career by first creating your digital assets. Your digital assets include, but not limited to, publishing your book and creating your first digital course.

I'll show precisely how-to pre-sell your expertise and then deliver on your promise inside of my signature program, The Income Amplifier. Discover the exact step-by-step strategy I used to launch my coaching services, and it earned me nearly $12,000 in just under one-week, with zero email subscribers. To learn more visit www.MollyAnnLuna.com/StepUp

ABOUT THE AUTHOR

Molly Ann is the life and business success strategist for the freedom focused entrepreneur who wants to do significant work and earn a handsome income.

She helps you pivot into your purpose, creates passive streams of income, and build True Wealth by using intelligent online marketing strategies inside of the Legacy Leaders Academy.

Her podcast, The Online Business Clinic provides easy-to-implement mini business blueprints to help entrepreneurs build a profitable and portable business without burnout.

Molly Ann is a U.S. Army Veteran and former Certified Financial Advisor who kicked corporate to the curb and successfully took her first business from $0 to 6-figures in just under 6-months.

She loves to travel for fun, and most weekends you can find her hiking near her home in sunny Las Vegas with her husband Jovan, two adorable kids, and their dog, Ridge.

www.ingramcontent.com/pod-product-compliance
Lightning Source LLC
Chambersburg PA
CBHW051539240526

45465CB00027B/725